Quackenbush appends instructions for the dancing game performed to this popular folksong at "play-parties" that flourished in the 1830's, and the bulk of the book, which includes ten of the 150 or so known verses, depicts one such party, celebrating sister Lou's engagement, where the flies in the buttermilk, cat in the cream jar, pig in the parlor, etc., create such havoc that the formally clad groom-to-be flees. But, as Quackenbush pictures it, Lou "found a partner, a better one too," and when last seen she is "off to Texas" on horseback with a bearded, fringed frontiersman. The easily followed story in pictures along with the potential for acting out gives *Skip to My Lou* more kick than many of Quackenbush's aggressively illustrated renditions of traditional American songs.
5–10, in groups

ROBERT QUACKENBUSH
SKIP TO MY LOU

J. B. LIPPINCOTT COMPANY/PHILADELPHIA AND NEW YORK

For Piet Robert,

Hansy, and Sheba—

those madcap dancers

U.S. Library of Congress Cataloging in Publication Data. Quackenbush, Robert M   Skip to my lou. SUM-
MARY: An illustrated version of ten verses from the traditional song telling how Lou loses her sweetheart,
finds another, and goes to Texas. Includes music and directions for dancing to the song. [1. Folk songs,
American] I. Title. PZ8.3.Q2Sk   784.4'973 [E]   74-14585   ISBN-0-397-31613-5

A NOTE

"Skip to My Lou" ("Lou" means "Sweetheart" in the South) is one of the most celebrated American folk songs. Its origin is unknown, but it was a favorite of the pioneers who traveled by flatboat down the winding Cumberland River in the late eighteenth century and settled the rich bottom lands of Kentucky and Tennessee.

By the 1830s the hard-working settlers had brought civilization to the area. Many of their homes were built and furnished in the fashionable Greek Revival style that had been introduced earlier by Thomas Jefferson. It is in this setting that Robert Quackenbush has chosen to illustrate "Skip to My Lou" as an engagement play-party. The play-party was a socially acceptable way to celebrate happy occasions despite stern religious prohibitions against "frivolous" entertainment. Though public dancing and fiddle music were considered by many as work of the devil, singing games could be enjoyed by all.

There are one hundred and fifty verses of "Skip to My Lou." Ten of the best known have been selected by the artist to tell his version of how Lou found a partner, lost him, then found another and went off to Texas. As an added attraction he has given each verse its own special chorus that can be acted out. He also includes the music and instructions for dancing the "Skip to My Lou."

This is Robert Quackenbush's sixth picture–song book of Americana for children. He invites everyone to join him at a rollicking party, circa 1832, when Kentucky and Tennessee were "outposts of civilization."

Dear Cousin George,
    Let me tell you about my
sister Lou's engagement party....

Flies in the buttermilk, shoo, shoo, shoo,
Flies in the buttermilk, shoo, shoo, shoo,
Flies in the buttermilk, shoo, shoo, shoo,
Skip to my Lou, my darling.

Buzz, buzz, skip to my Lou,
Buzz, buzz, skip to my Lou,
Buzz, buzz, skip to my Lou,
Skip to my Lou, my darling.

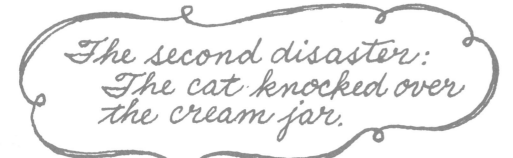

The second disaster:
The cat knocked over
the cream jar.

Cat's in the cream jar, ooh, ooh, ooh,
Cat's in the cream jar, ooh, ooh, ooh,
Cat's in the cream jar, ooh, ooh, ooh,
    Skip to my Lou, my darling.

Meow, meow, skip to my Lou,
Meow, meow, skip to my Lou,
Meow, meow, skip to my Lou,
    Skip to my Lou, my darling.

The third disaster:
My mice ate the
party sandwiches.

Mice in the bread tray, how they chew,
Mice in the bread tray, how they chew,
Mice in the bread tray, how they chew,
    Skip to my Lou, my darling.

Squeak, squeak, skip to my Lou,
Squeak, squeak, skip to my Lou,
Squeak, squeak, skip to my Lou,
    Skip to my Lou, my darling.

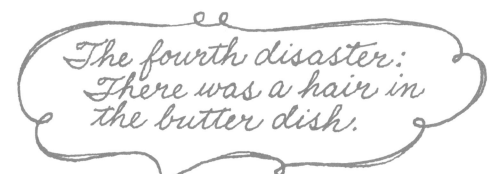

The fourth disaster:
There was a hair in
the butter dish.

Hair in the butter dish, six feet long,
Hair in the butter dish, six feet long,
Hair in the butter dish, six feet long,
Skip to my Lou, my darling.

Ick, ick, skip to my Lou,
Ick, ick, skip to my Lou,
Ick, ick, skip to my Lou,
Skip to my Lou, my darling.

The fifth disaster:
Pigs ran through
the parlor.

Pig's in the parlor, what'll we do?
Pig's in the parlor, what'll we do?
Pig's in the parlor, what'll we do?
    Skip to my Lou, my darling.

Oink, oink, skip to my Lou,
Oink, oink, skip to my Lou,
Oink, oink, skip to my Lou,
Skip to my Lou, my darling.

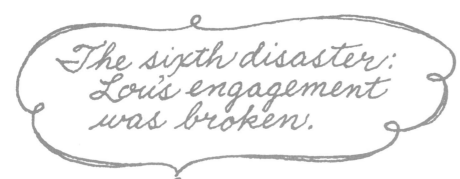

The sixth disaster:
Lou's engagement
was broken.

Lost my partner, what'll I do?
Lost my partner, what'll I do?
Lost my partner, what'll I do?
Skip to my Lou, my darling.

Boo, hoo, skip to my Lou,
Boo, hoo, skip to my Lou,
Boo, hoo, skip to my Lou,
Skip to my Lou, my darling.

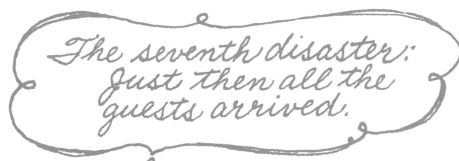

The seventh disaster:
Just then all the
guests arrived.

Hurry up slowpokes, do, oh, do,
Hurry up slowpokes, do, oh, do,
Hurry up slowpokes, do, oh, do,
Skip to my Lou, my darling.

Hop, hop, skip to my Lou,
Hop, hop, skip to my Lou,
Hop, hop, skip to my Lou,
Skip to my Lou, my darling.

The eighth disaster:
Lou found a new sweetheart.
Father didn't approve.

Found a partner, a better one too,
Found a partner, a better one too,
Found a partner, a better one too,
Skip to my Lou, my darling.

Coo, coo, skip to my Lou,
Coo, coo, skip to my Lou,
Coo, coo, skip to my Lou,
Skip to my Lou, my darling.

The ninth disaster:
The guests wouldn't
go home.

We'll keep it up till half past two,
We'll keep it up till half past two,
We'll keep it up till half past two,
Skip to my Lou, my darling.

Tick, tock, skip to my Lou,
Tick, tock, skip to my Lou,
Tick, tock, skip to my Lou,
Skip to my Lou, my darling.

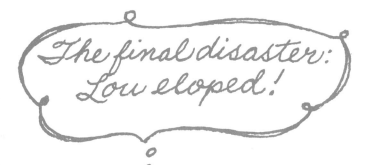

The final disaster:
Lou eloped!

Off to Texas, two by two,
Off to Texas, two by two,
Off to Texas, two by two,
Skip to my Lou, my darling.

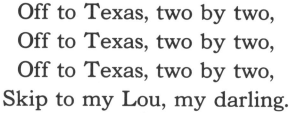

Skip, skip, skip to my Lou,
Skip, skip, skip to my Lou,
Skip, skip, skip to my Lou,
Skip to my Lou, my darling.

Your Cousin,
Matthew
P.S. It was a disastrous
party, but it sure was fun!

SKIP TO MY LOU

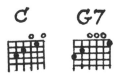

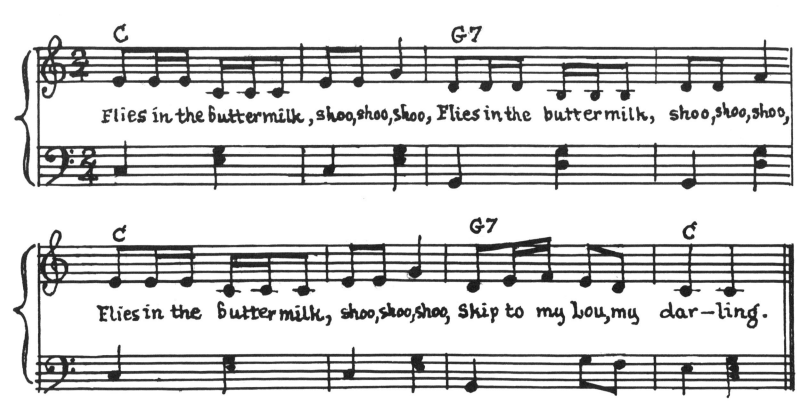

Flies in the buttermilk, shoo, shoo, shoo, Flies in the buttermilk, shoo, shoo, shoo,

Flies in the buttermilk, shoo, shoo, shoo, Skip to my Lou, my dar-ling.

Here's how to dance the "Skip to My Lou" the way it was done at play-parties in 1832.

HOW TO DANCE THE "SKIP TO MY LOU"

1. The "Skip to My Lou" is danced by any number of couples, plus one player without a partner. The couples form a circle, facing in, with the single player in the center. If boy-girl couples are playing, boys stand to the right of their partners.

2. Everyone sings the first verse, clapping hands, and at the end the player in the center "steals" a partner.

3. This new couple skips around the outside of the circle, both hands joined (right hands crossed over left hands), while the chorus is sung. Singers can act out the choruses (Example: pretend you are a mouse for "Squeak, squeak").

4. The player whose partner was taken goes into the center, as the new couple takes that place in the circle. At the end of the second verse, the single player "steals" a new partner. Repeat for every verse.